LIVE LIKE A
ROMAN

DISCOVERING THE SECRETS OF ANCIENT ROME

CLAIRE SAUNDERS

ILLUSTRATED BY
RUTH HICKSON

Button
BOOKS

CONTENTS

WHO WERE THE ROMANS?

Ancient Rome was one of the greatest and most powerful civilisations in history. It lasted for over a thousand years, growing from a small settlement, on the banks of the River Tiber in Italy, into a vast Empire that ruled much of Europe.

Rome

The Roman Empire

At its biggest, around 2,000 years ago, Rome's empire was home to more than 50 million people. Some lived in the great capital city of Rome, others in bustling African ports, tiny villages in Gaul, thriving Syrian/near Eastern cities or windswept army camps in Britain. With each new land the Romans conquered, they spread their culture, ideas and language far and wide.

The key to Rome's success was its powerful, well-trained army.

Finding evidence

The Romans left behind lots of evidence about their lives, from statues and wall paintings to coins, letters, poetry and even rude graffiti! One of the places that has taught archaeologists a lot about Roman life is the town of Pompeii, in southern Italy. In 79 CE, a volcano called Mount Vesuvius erupted, burying Pompeii under a layer of ash. This perfectly preserved the town as it was on that day, frozen in time.

Pompeii artefacts

A Roman friend

My name is Tiro. I am eight years old and I have been a slave since I was born. I live in my master's house with my sister and my mother. I have to work hard but my master and mistress are kind and I am treated well. One day I hope to earn my freedom. Have you been to my city before? I want to tell you all about the banquet my master hosted last week, and my trip to the chariot races! Come with me and let me share some stories about my life.

The Roman legacy

Although the Romans lived a long time ago, many of their ideas and inventions are part of our way of life today.

Concrete

The Roman's invention of concrete allowed them to build super-strong structures such as aqueducts, bridges and other buildings. Some are still standing 2,000 years later.

MAGRIPPA·L·F·COS·TERTIVM·FECIT

The Pantheon, Rome

Alcántara bridge, Spain

Underfloor heating

Just like us, the Romans had a form of underfloor heating. Their invention was called the hypocaust, and was used to heat bathhouses (see page 26) and the homes of wealthy Romans (see page 20).

The modern calendar

The calendar we use, with 365 days and a leap year every four years, was brought in by Julius Caesar in 46 BCE. One month was renamed Julius (July) in his honour. The other months are named after Roman gods, Roman numbers and the emperor Augustus (August).

Language and alphabet

The Roman language, called Latin, isn't spoken anymore. But many languages across Europe developed from it, including French, Spanish and Italian. Many more languages, including English, use the Roman alphabet. It's the most widely used writing system in the world.

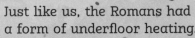

PER·ARDVA· AD·ASTRA·

The Romans only had 23 letters in their alphabet. J, U and W were added later.

TIMELINE OF ANCIENT ROME

The history of ancient Rome covers more than a thousand years. In its earliest days it was ruled by kings. Then it became a republic, with power held by elected officials. After that, came Rome's golden age under the emperors. What had once been a small city of wooden huts was now a powerful empire!

509 BCE
The last king is overthrown and Rome becomes a republic, governed by a group called the Senate. Its leaders are elected by the people.

30 BCE
Rome defeats Queen Cleopatra VII in Egypt.

c.753–509 BCE
The city is ruled by kings.

The Republic (509–27 BCE)

Early Rome (753–509 BCE)

343–146 BCE
Rome takes control of Italy, and then conquers Greece, Spain and northern Africa.

753 BCE
According to legend, Rome is founded by Romulus, the son of Mars (the god of war). In the story, Romulus and his twin brother Remus are abandoned and raised by a she-wolf. Romulus kills his brother and becomes the first king, giving the city its name.

49 BCE
After conquering Gaul, the general Julius Caesar seizes power and makes himself a dictator. He is murdered soon afterwards.

27 BCE–14 CE
Caesar Augustus becomes the first emperor. He is one of Rome's most successful leaders.

From 285 CE
Emperor Diocletian splits the Empire into two – a western half and an eastern half – to make it easier to rule.

476 CE
The last emperor of the Western Roman Empire, Romulus Augustulus, is overthrown by Germanic tribes.

98–117 CE
Under the rule of soldier-emperor Trajan, the Roman Empire reaches its largest size.

Imperial Rome
(27 BCE–476 CE)

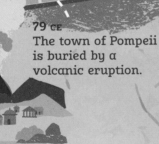

79 CE
The town of Pompeii is buried by a volcanic eruption.

235–284 CE
The Empire is weakened by barbarian tribes attacking from the north and east.

312 CE
Constantine becomes the first Christian emperor.

Mad, bad emperors

Caligula (37–41 CE) demanded to be treated like a god, and put people to death for no reason.

Nero (54–68 CE) murdered his mother and wife and was said to have started the Great Fire of Rome on purpose.

Commodus (176–192 CE) liked to dress up as a gladiator and kill defenceless wild beasts.

MAP OF THE ROMAN EMPIRE

Rome's empire covered most of Europe and the lands around the Mediterranean Sea. The Romans divided the land they conquered into areas called provinces. This map shows the Roman Empire at its greatest size, in the early 2nd century CE.

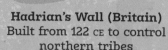

Hadrian's Wall (Britain)
Built from 122 CE to control northern tribes

Britannia (Britain)

Londinium (London)

Colonia Claudia Ara Agrippinensium (now Cologne)

Leather
Metals
Pork
Wine

Gallia (Gaul)

Baths, Aquae Sulis (Bath, England)
Built in the 1st century CE

Hispania (Spain)

Italia (Italy)

Rome

Olive oil
Metals
Dried fish

Mare Internum (Mediterranean Sea)

Pont du Gard aqueduct (France)
Built in the 1st century CE

Gades (now Cadiz)

Roman Theatre of Orange (France)
Built in 40 BCE

Carthage

Grain
Ivory
Oil
Wild animals
Cotton

Africa

Most big cities in the Roman Empire were by the sea or rivers. Everywhere was connected by a big network of roads built by the Romans.

Latin was the official language of the Roman Empire. Some places around Europe have kept their Latin name, for example London (Londinium).

The Romans used the term 'barbarians' to describe groups of people who lived outside the Empire, such as the Goths, Vandals, Franks, Saxons and Huns.

The provinces sent taxes, slaves, food and materials to Rome and made it very rich. The map shows some of the goods that were sent to Rome.

Key:
Roman Empire ▪
Trade route ◁····
Places of interest ●
Cities ●

Pula Arena (Croatia)
Built in the 1st century CE

Herculaneum ruins (Italy)
Buried when Mount Vesuvius erupted in 79 CE, along with nearby Pompeii

Byzantium
(later Constantinople, now Istanbul)

Asia

Grain
Spices
Ivory
Silk

Marble   Ephesus

Antioch

Athens

Library of Celsus, Ephesus (Turkey)
Built in the 2nd century CE. Ephesus was an important port.

Colosseum (Rome)
Opened in 80 CE

Alexandria
Aegyptus (Egypt)

Ivory
Dried fish
Cotton
Papyrus
Grain

The provinces used the same coins and language as the Romans, but they kept some of their own culture and customs too, like local calendars and religions.

ROMAN SOCIETY

Not all Romans lived the same way. The rights and privileges a person had depended on which group in society they belonged to. There were three main groups: citizens, non-citizens (people who came from outside Rome) and slaves. Citizens had the most rights, and slaves had none at all.

Citizens

Being a Roman male citizen gave certain rights, such as being allowed to vote, own property and serve in government. It also gave men the right to wear a toga, Rome's formal national dress. Citizens were divided into the different ranks shown in the pyramid.

Emperor

At the top was the **emperor**, who had absolute power. Some were fair rulers, but others were terrible tyrants (see page 7).

Then came the **senators**, important and wealthy men who served in the Senate (the governing assembly). The two most important senators were the consuls.

A non-citizen could gain citizenship in a few different ways, including by serving in the army for 25 years.

Senators

Just below senators were wealthy men called **equestrians**.

The lowest ranking citizens were **plebeians**. They were ordinary people like shopkeepers, legionaries, craftsmen and labourers.

Most citizens were plebeians. Only a tiny number of Romans were rich.

Equestrians

Plebeians

Slaves

Over a quarter of the people in ancient Rome were slaves. They might have been captured in war, abandoned at birth or born into slavery to slave parents. Slaves had no rights and were the property of their owners. Some had a terrible life, especially those forced to work long days as labourers on farms or in dangerous mines underground. But others were treated well, especially those who worked in skilled jobs like teaching.

Freedom!

Some slaves were able to earn their freedom and be set free. If a freed slave was owned by a citizen, they became a citizen too, and so did their children after them. Emperor Pertinax, who ruled for three months in 193 CE, was the son of a freed slave!

Household slaves

Teacher

Miner

The rights of women

Roman women didn't have the same rights as men. Female citizens were not allowed to vote or hold any positions of power. They were expected to be good wives and mothers, and to marry who they were told to. Very few girls were educated and most jobs were for men.

A few women did become powerful by using their influence over their husbands or sons. Julia Agrippina was one of the most powerful women in Rome. She was the sister of Emperor Caligula, the wife of Emperor Claudius and the mother of Emperor Nero.

Julia Agrippina

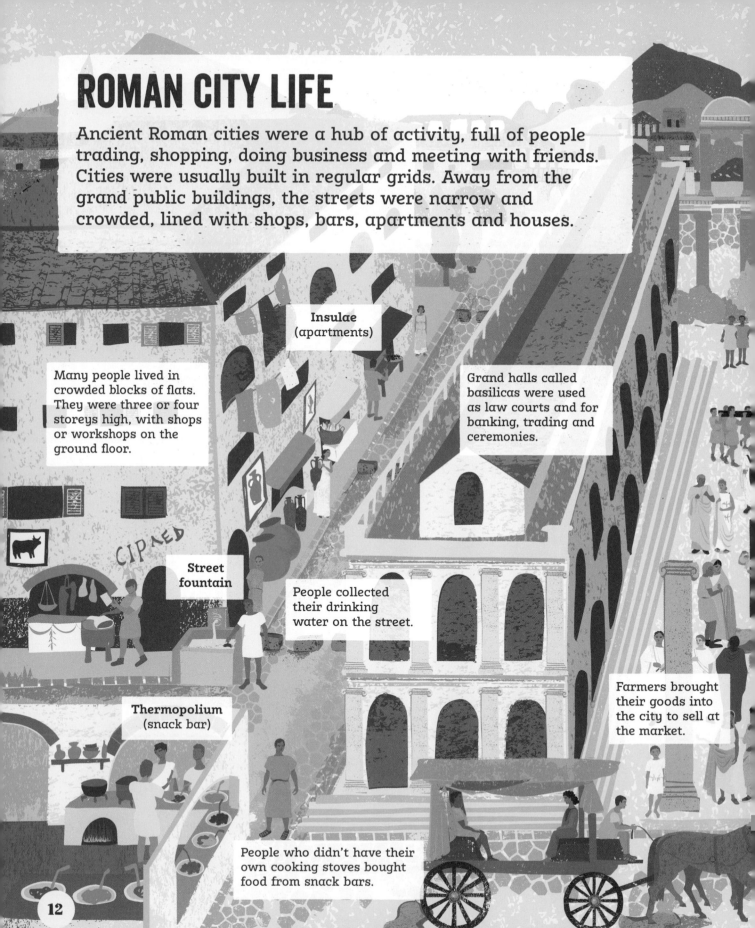

ROMAN CITY LIFE

Ancient Roman cities were a hub of activity, full of people trading, shopping, doing business and meeting with friends. Cities were usually built in regular grids. Away from the grand public buildings, the streets were narrow and crowded, lined with shops, bars, apartments and houses.

**Insulae
(apartments)**

Many people lived in crowded blocks of flats. They were three or four storeys high, with shops or workshops on the ground floor.

Grand halls called basilicas were used as law courts and for banking, trading and ceremonies.

Street fountain

People collected their drinking water on the street.

**Thermopolium
(snack bar)**

Farmers brought their goods into the city to sell at the market.

People who didn't have their own cooking stoves bought food from snack bars.

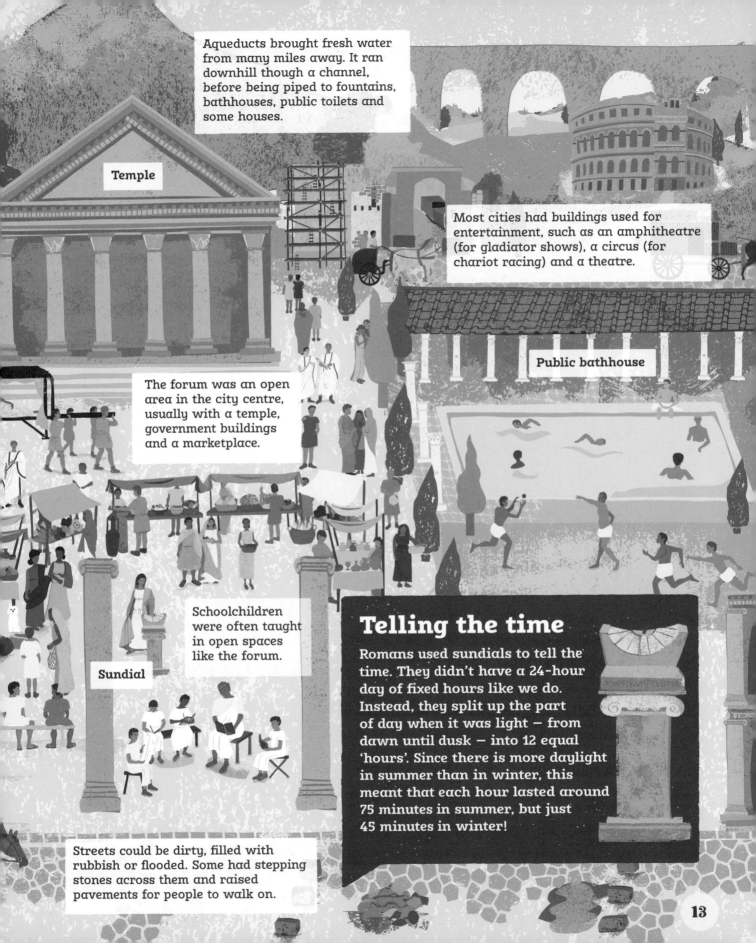

Aqueducts brought fresh water from many miles away. It ran downhill though a channel, before being piped to fountains, bathhouses, public toilets and some houses.

Temple

Most cities had buildings used for entertainment, such as an amphitheatre (for gladiator shows), a circus (for chariot racing) and a theatre.

Public bathhouse

The forum was an open area in the city centre, usually with a temple, government buildings and a marketplace.

Schoolchildren were often taught in open spaces like the forum.

Sundial

Streets could be dirty, filled with rubbish or flooded. Some had stepping stones across them and raised pavements for people to walk on.

Telling the time

Romans used sundials to tell the time. They didn't have a 24-hour day of fixed hours like we do. Instead, they split up the part of day when it was light – from dawn until dusk – into 12 equal 'hours'. Since there is more daylight in summer than in winter, this meant that each hour lasted around 75 minutes in summer, but just 45 minutes in winter!

EVERYDAY JOBS

There were lots of different jobs in ancient Rome: farmers, shopkeepers, merchants, lawyers, government officials, soldiers, engineers, labourers, politicians, musicians, actors, even armpit-hair pluckers! Most jobs were for men, but some women worked as hairdressers or midwives, or helped their husbands.

Engineers

The Romans were very skilful engineers. They improved on the ideas and techniques of people who had come before them to construct impressive aqueducts, arched bridges, roads, tunnels, mills, mines, weapons and more. These all helped to make Rome rich and powerful.

Craftsmen

Skilled craftsmen provided people with everything they couldn't make themselves, from clothes and shoes to pottery and furniture. They often lived above their workshops, and their family helped them with the work.

There was no such thing as retirement, unless you were in the army. Most people worked until they died.

Time off

The working day began when it got light. Wealthier Romans finished work at lunchtime, leaving the afternoon free for relaxing at the baths. Craftsmen and shopkeepers worked a little later. The Romans didn't have weekends. Every day was a working day, except for festival days.

Farmers

Most ordinary Romans lived in the countryside, growing crops such as grapes and olives, or rearing animals. Many farmers were slaves who worked on huge estates owned by rich Romans. The days were long and exhausting.

Coins

Roman coins were used for buying and selling goods all over the Empire. They usually had a picture of the emperor on one side. This was a good way to show off his image to millions of people in faraway provinces.

Farmers used a curved tool called a sickle to harvest their crops.

Shopkeepers

Shopkeepers sold goods such as cloth, meat, cheese and wine from small rooms on the ground floor of houses. Most Romans bought their bread from a bakery, rather than making it at home. Bakers first ground the grain into flour, then baked the bread in round ovens.

Wash your clothes Roman-style!

Working in a laundry was one of the hardest and stinkiest jobs in ancient Rome. The workers (called fullers) soaked clothes in tubs of old urine and trod on them to get all the dirt out. Try washing your clothes the same way (but without the urine!). Put a piece of clothing in a bath or bowl with some soapy water and squish it with your feet, then rinse it clean.

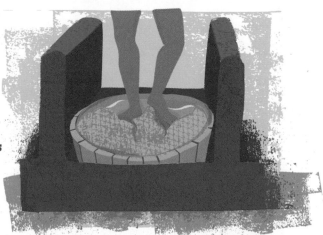

MAKE AN ABACUS

Merchants, engineers and other people dealing with numbers used a type of ancient calculator called an abacus. The Romans developed their own version of this, which was small so it could be easily carried around. It had a metal frame, with beads in grooves that could be slid up and down to do calculations.

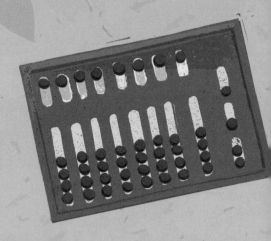

You will need

- **6 large lollipop sticks**
- **3 wooden skewers**, cut into 6 lengths of 4in (10cm)
- **30 pony beads** (or other small beads) with a $5/32$in (4mm) hole
- **Glue gun** or craft glue
- **Pen**

1 Glue one end of each of the skewers onto a lollipop stick. Make sure they are evenly spaced.

2 When the glue is dry, thread a bead onto each skewer. Glue a second lollipop stick underneath the first, about ¾in (2cm) below it.

3 Once the glue is dry, thread four beads onto each skewer. Then attach the third lollipop stick along the bottom.

4 Glue three more lollipop sticks over the top of the first three.

5 Once the glue is dry, write on the Roman numerals. From right to left these are:
I (ones)
X (tens)
C (hundreds)
M (thousands)
$\overline{X}$ (tens of thousands)
$\overline{C}$ (hundreds of thousands)

Roman numerals

The Romans didn't use the numbers we use today (1, 2, 3, and so on). They used letters to stand for numbers instead. There were just seven symbols:

I = 1	C = 100
V = 5	D = 500
X = 10	M = 1,000
L = 50	

To make all the other numbers, they added together or subtracted the symbols from each other.

If a smaller symbol appeared after a larger symbol, it was added to it, so VI was 6 (5 + 1).

But if a smaller symbol appeared before a larger symbol, it was subtracted, so IV was 4 (5 − 1).

How complicated! The system meant that numbers got very long very quickly. For example, the Romans wrote 2,888 as MMDCCCLXXXVIII.

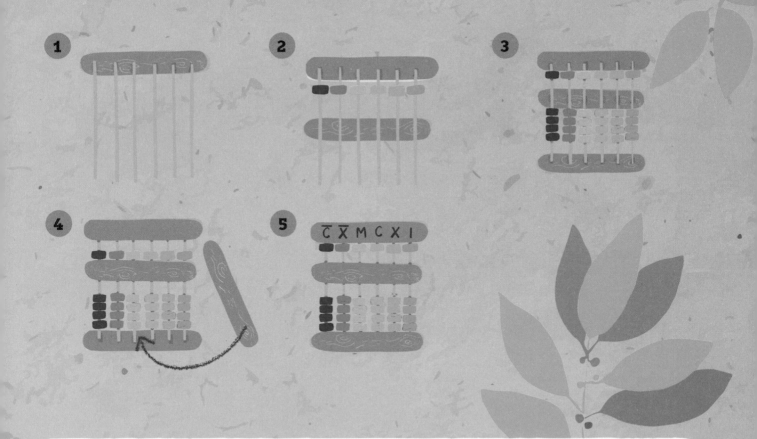

How it works

Each column of the abacus has a value. The farthest column on the right is the 'ones' (1–9), the one next to it is the 'tens' (10–90), then the 'hundreds' (100–900), and so on.

Before you start, make sure the single bead is pushed to the top of the abacus, and the four beads are pushed to the bottom.

To count a number, move the beads to the centre of the abacus. The beads on the top are worth 5, and those on the bottom are worth 1. There are two examples shown on the right. The top drawing shows the number 7 and the bottom, the number 71.

To make the number 7:
In the 'ones' column, push one bead down from the top (worth 5), and two beads up from the bottom (worth 1 each): 5 + 2 = 7.

To make the number 71: In the 'tens' column, push one bead down (worth 50) and two beads up (worth 10 each). In the 'ones' column, push one bead up from the bottom.

A DAY IN THE LIFE OF A ROMAN SLAVE

The day started early in ancient Rome, whether you were a rich senator or a slave. This is what might have happened to our slave boy in the 12 Roman 'hours' of daylight (see page 13).

First hour: wake up

He wakes up at dawn and has a quick wash.

Help the master

He brings water so that his master can wash his face, then helps him put on his heavy, cumbersome toga. His master will have a proper wash at the bathhouse later.

Second hour: house jobs

After a piece of bread and a cup of water for breakfast, it's time to help clean the house. He empties the chamber pots and clears the ashes from the charcoal braziers.

Sweeping and dusting doesn't take long as there isn't much furniture.

Do the washing up Roman-style!

The Romans didn't have detergent to wash their dishes with. Instead, they used sand to scour away the food and grease, and then rinsed everything clean with water. Give it a go, using coarse sea salt instead of sand. How well does it work?

Fourth hour: the market

With an older slave, he heads to the market. Today they have to buy wine, fresh fish and bread. The mistress tells them to pick up the master's clean togas from the fuller's at the same time.

Fifth hour: public toilets

He needs to use the toilet, so he pops to the public ones. They're a bit stinky, but better than using the street. He wipes his bottom with a sponge on a stick, called an xylospongium, that's shared by everyone and then rinsed after use.

Sixth hour: lunch

After eating some bread and cheese for lunch, he has some free time to play knucklebones with his little sister. She's such a cheat but he lets her win anyway.

Seventh hour: fetching water

The cook tells him to go to the fountain to fetch water. It's hot, hard work carrying a heavy pot of water through the streets. Soon he won't have to do this job, because pipes are being laid that will carry fresh water straight to the house – he can't wait!

Ninth hour: dinner

It's time to serve dinner. He helps carry the dishes into the dining room and pours the wine while he listens to the master telling his wife about his day at the law courts. Afterwards, he helps wash up the dishes and eats dinner with his mother and sister.

Twelfth hour: time to sleep

It's getting dark and everyone in the house is going to bed. He's so tired! He sleeps in his tunic, so all he needs to do is unroll a mattress in the storeroom and pull a blanket over himself. His mother kisses him goodnight and soon he's asleep.

INSIDE A ROMAN HOUSE

Wealthy Romans lived in a town house called a domus, which was beautifully decorated with mosaics and wall paintings. It was a busy place, with lots of people coming and going. In the morning, the master welcomed business visitors, and later there might be guests for dinner. All day long, the family was surrounded by their many slaves.

Important business guests would be invited into the study.

Every home had a small shrine where the family made daily offerings to the gods of the house.

The first room through the front door was a large hall that was open to the sky. Most meetings with visitors took place here, so it had to look impressive.

The floor was made of marble or mosaics, and walls were painted in rich, bright colours.

The rooms at the front of the house were rented out and used as shops.

Lararium (shrine)

Thermopolium (snack bar)

Atrium (entrance hall)

Taberna (shop)

Roman pets

Romans loved their pets, especially their dogs. They also kept caged birds and fish, as well as pet snakes to kill the rats and mice in the house.

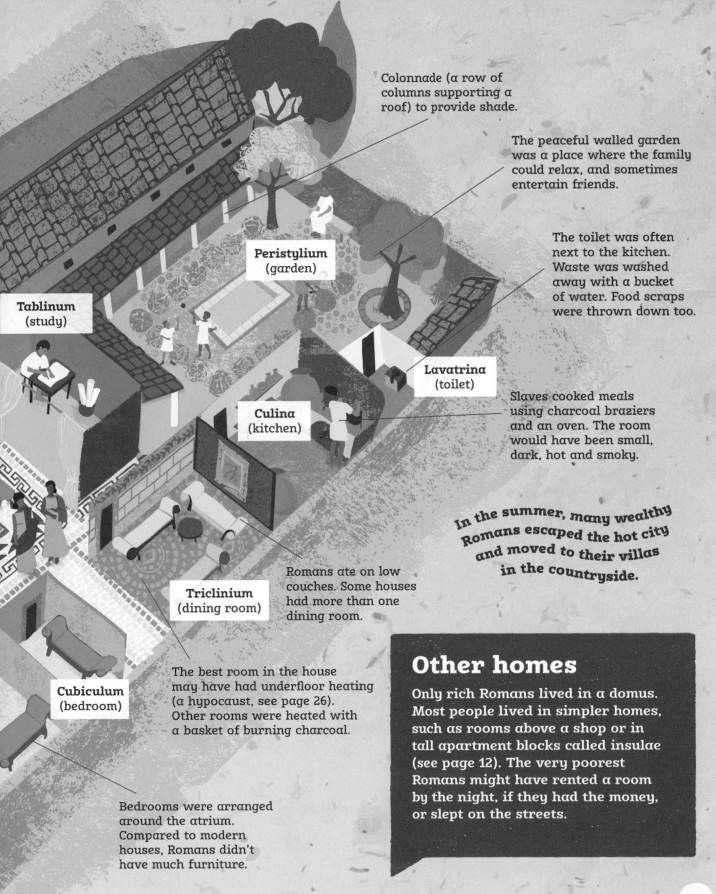

Colonnade (a row of columns supporting a roof) to provide shade.

The peaceful walled garden was a place where the family could relax, and sometimes entertain friends.

The toilet was often next to the kitchen. Waste was washed away with a bucket of water. Food scraps were thrown down too.

Peristylium (garden)

Tablinum (study)

Lavatrina (toilet)

Slaves cooked meals using charcoal braziers and an oven. The room would have been small, dark, hot and smoky.

Culina (kitchen)

In the summer, many wealthy Romans escaped the hot city and moved to their villas in the countryside.

Romans ate on low couches. Some houses had more than one dining room.

Triclinium (dining room)

Other homes

Only rich Romans lived in a domus. Most people lived in simpler homes, such as rooms above a shop or in tall apartment blocks called insulae (see page 12). The very poorest Romans might have rented a room by the night, if they had the money, or slept on the streets.

The best room in the house may have had underfloor heating (a hypocaust, see page 26). Other rooms were heated with a basket of burning charcoal.

Cubiculum (bedroom)

Bedrooms were arranged around the atrium. Compared to modern houses, Romans didn't have much furniture.

CHILDHOOD AND FAMILY LIFE

The head of the Roman household was the paterfamilias, the oldest male of the family (usually the father). He owned all property, arranged the children's marriages and even had the power to abandon or sell his children into slavery. Women were in charge of running the home and bringing up children.

Going to school

Children from wealthy families started school when they were about six or seven. Some were taught at home by tutors, and others went to schools set up in rented rooms or in the open air. School was taught seven days a week, but children did get time off in the summer and on festival days – phew!

Schools were very strict. Children could get beaten if they made a mistake or misbehaved.

Playing with toys

Roman toys weren't all that different to toys today. Children played with dolls, balls, wooden swords and pull-along toys. When boys were around 14, they gave up their toys at a special ceremony to mark the end of their childhood. Girls did the same the night before their wedding.

Hard work

Not all children got an education. Girls were only taught the basics, and then had to learn household skills instead. They were expected to marry when they were around 14. Children in poorer families didn't go to school at all but had to start work as soon as they were able, generally when they were between five and ten.

MAKE KNUCKLEBONES

Romans young and old liked playing with knucklebones, game pieces made from sheep's or goat's bones. Children played a catching game with them, while adults used them as dice for gambling.

You will need

- **Air-dry clay**, around ¾oz (20g)
- **Ruler**
- **Blunt knife**
- **Marker pen**

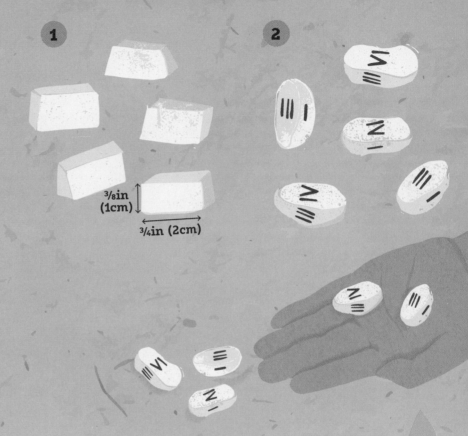

1 Cut out five rectangular pieces of clay, each ¾in (2cm) long, ⅜in (1cm) wide and ⅜in (1cm) thick. Smooth the clay at the corners, so the knucklebones can't stand on their ends. Leave to dry.

2 Once dry, write these Roman numerals on the four long sides: I (one), III (three), IV (four) and VI (six).

How to play

Knucklebones were played with in lots of different ways. Try out these games with a friend.

1. Throw four of the bones on the ground. Then throw the fifth bone in the air, and before it reaches the ground, pick up one of the bones. Do the same thing again, but this time try to pick up two bones. Next, scoop up three bones, and finally all four bones.

2. Take turns trying to throw the bones into a small container, like an empty jam jar.

3. Use the bones like dice. Each throw, add up the Roman numerals and keep a note of your score. Who can score the highest with three throws?

MAKE A WAX TABLET

Roman papyrus paper was expensive, so instead schoolchildren used a wax tablet called a tabula to write on. This could be used again and again by smoothing over the marks. Have a go at making your own tabula. This one uses modelling clay, but see the box opposite for a version that uses wax.

You will need

- Cardboard
- Scissors
- Ruler and pencil
- Glue
- 7oz (200g) non-drying white modelling clay (or you could use yellow to look like beeswax)
- Rolling pin
- Blunt knife
- Brown poster paint

1 Cut out two book-sized pieces of cardboard. On one piece, draw a rectangle around ¾in (2cm) in from the edges, and cut it out.

2 Glue the two pieces of cardboard together to make a frame.

3 Roll out the modelling clay using a rolling pin and lay it over the tablet, pressing down gently around the edges of the frame.

4 Run a blunt knife around the edge of the frame to cut away the excess clay.

5 Paint the cardboard brown to look like wood, then leave to dry. You can write on your tablet using any tool with a sharp point, such as a pencil or a wooden skewer. To erase a mark, simply smooth the clay with your finger.

It wasn't just schoolchildren who used wax tablets. Adults used them too, for recording information and writing letters.

Using a tabula

The Roman tabula was a book-sized piece of wood with a shallow recess on one side, which was filled with a thin layer of beeswax. A sharp tool called a stylus was used to scratch into the wax. Marks could be erased using the blunt end of the stylus, or by heating up the wax to melt it. Sometimes two or more tablets were tied together to make a booklet.

1

2

3

4

5

Important documents and books were written with ink on papyrus (made from reeds) or parchment (made from animal skins).

Wax alternative

You'll need an adult to help with this version of the tablet.

Follow steps 1 and 2 above to make the cardboard frame. Then put 3½oz (100g) wax flakes in a heatproof jug and place it in a pan partly filled with water. Heat the water on the stove, keeping an eye on the wax. Once it is melted, carefully remove the jug from the saucepan and allow it to cool for a few minutes.

Pour a thin layer of wax into the cardboard frame. Allow this to cool and set for five minutes, before pouring another thin layer on top. Leave the wax to cool and harden.

You can write on your tablet using something sharp, such as a pencil or a wooden skewer. Press gently into the wax. To erase a mark, rub the wax with your finger or scrape it using a blunt knife. To wipe the whole tablet clean, ask an adult to heat a blunt knife in some hot water, then run it over the surface to melt it slightly and make it smooth again.

ROMAN BATHS

Very few Roman houses had baths, but almost every town had a public bathhouse. People went there every day to wash, exercise, stroll in the gardens, play games, meet with friends and do business – some bathhouses even had libraries and lecture halls! Entry was cheap, so everyone could afford to go.

Clothes were left in niches set into the walls. Slaves kept a watchful eye over people's belongings.

People visited the warm room in between the hot and cold rooms. They could relax here, chat and have massages.

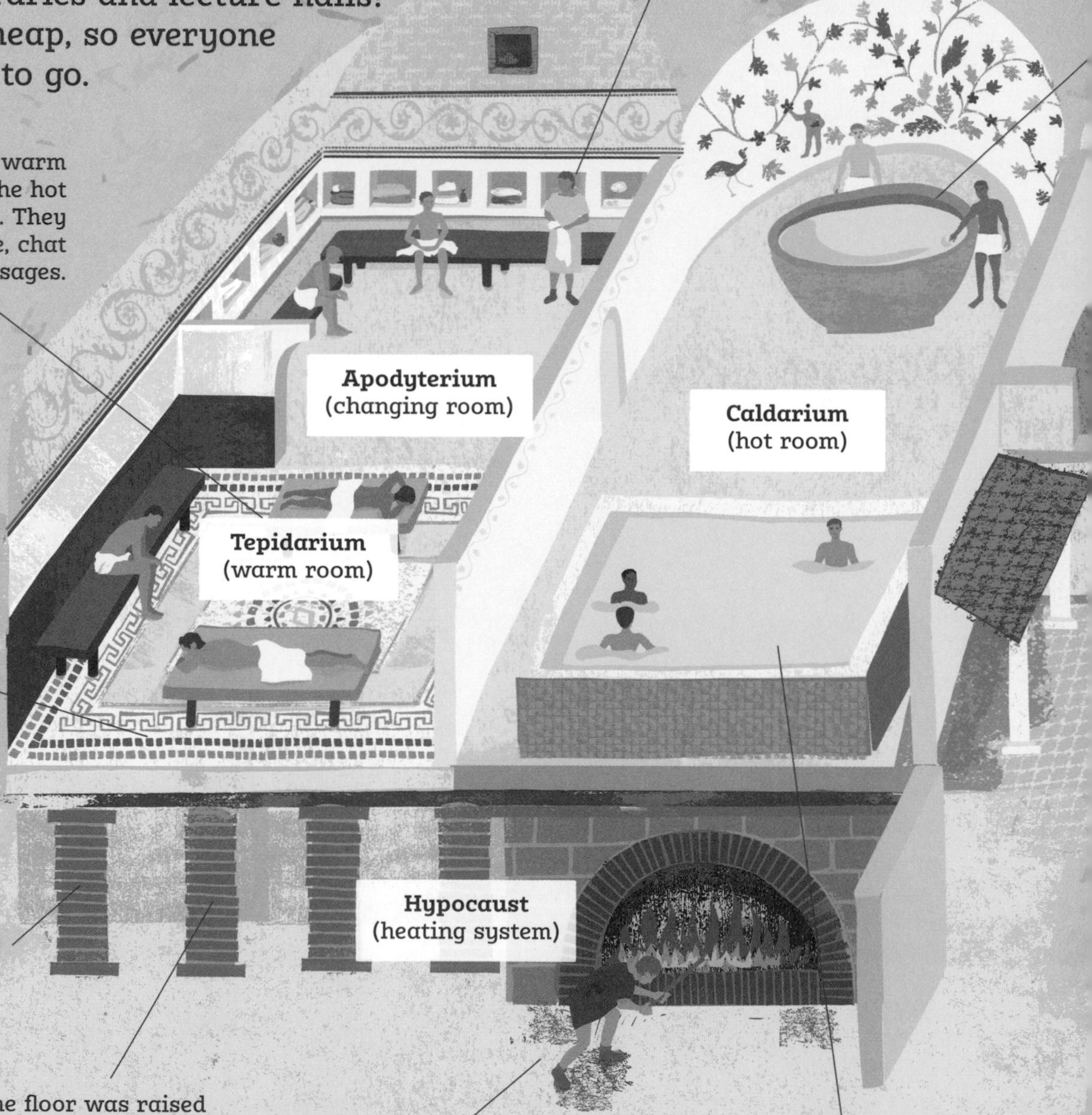

Apodyterium (changing room)

Caldarium (hot room)

Tepidarium (warm room)

The heated floor could become very hot and be difficult to stand on in bare feet!

The bathhouse used an underfloor heating system called a hypocaust to heat its rooms.

Hypocaust (heating system)

The floor was raised up on brick columns, so that hot air from a furnace could flow underneath it.

Slaves kept the furnace burning – an awful job that would have been unbearably hot.

Hot bath for a relaxing soak.

Large tub of hot water, which bathers could sprinkle on themselves.

Frigidarium (cold room)

Visits often ended with a plunge in a cold pool. Brrr!

Visiting the baths

Bathhouses had several rooms of different temperatures, which people moved between. Men and women had separate areas in the baths, or went at different times of day. Men normally visited in the afternoon, after work.

Some baths had a big pool for swimming.

Palaestra (exercise area)

Bathers lifted weights, played ball games, ran or wrestled and rolled a metal or wooden hoop with a stick.

Clean yourself Roman-style

Romans didn't use soap. Instead, they rubbed scented oil onto their skin, and then scraped off the dirt using a curved metal tool called a strigil. Slaves usually did this for them. You can have a go at cleaning yourself the way the Romans did, using a lollipop stick as a home-made strigil. First, smear a bit of dirt on your arm or leg. Then rub in some olive oil and scrape it off with a lollipop stick, before rinsing with water. How well did your strigil remove the dirt?

Strigils and oil flask

AT THE BATHS

Today I am going with my master to the bathhouse. The sun is still hot but the shadows are lengthening when we set off from home. Sometimes the master likes to be carried in a litter but today he wants to walk. I think he's feeling cheerful because he had some good news at the law courts. He'll be looking forward to telling his friends all about it. My master has brought a few of us slaves with him today – Felix is carrying his strigil and oil, and Gallio has come along to guard the clothes in the changing room. Last month the master's pouch of coins went missing and he wasn't happy. I have an important job too, carrying the towels.

We turn the corner and I can hear singing, splashing and shouting – we're there! We make our way to the apodyterium, where Gallio helps the master get changed. We look for an empty niche to put his clothes in while my master heads to the tepidarium for a massage.

Afterwards we follow the master to the palaestra, where a few men are lifting weights and wrestling. My master joins two of his friends playing a game, throwing a ball to each other quickly and without warning. Every time they drop it they shout and laugh, and I have to run to pick it up. It's fun to watch but I wish they wouldn't drop it so often.

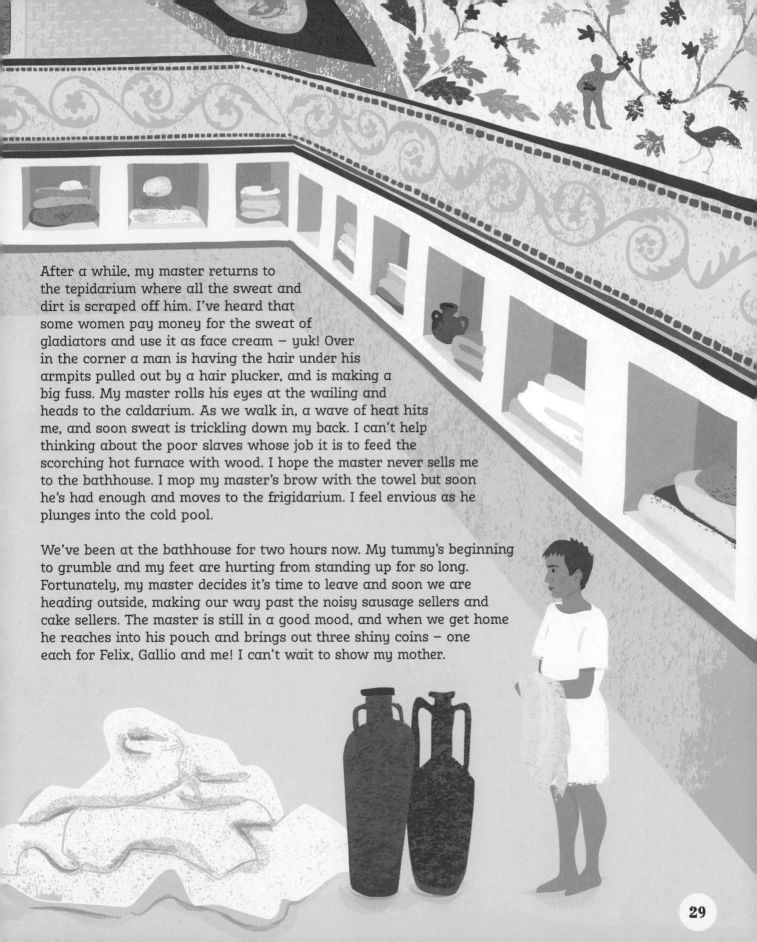

After a while, my master returns to the tepidarium where all the sweat and dirt is scraped off him. I've heard that some women pay money for the sweat of gladiators and use it as face cream – yuk! Over in the corner a man is having the hair under his armpits pulled out by a hair plucker, and is making a big fuss. My master rolls his eyes at the wailing and heads to the caldarium. As we walk in, a wave of heat hits me, and soon sweat is trickling down my back. I can't help thinking about the poor slaves whose job it is to feed the scorching hot furnace with wood. I hope the master never sells me to the bathhouse. I mop my master's brow with the towel but soon he's had enough and moves to the frigidarium. I feel envious as he plunges into the cold pool.

We've been at the bathhouse for two hours now. My tummy's beginning to grumble and my feet are hurting from standing up for so long. Fortunately, my master decides it's time to leave and soon we are heading outside, making our way past the noisy sausage sellers and cake sellers. The master is still in a good mood, and when we get home he reaches into his pouch and brings out three shiny coins – one each for Felix, Gallio and me! I can't wait to show my mother.

ROMAN FASHION

Most people in ancient Rome wore the same thing – a simple tunic. On formal occasions like business meetings or a trip to the theatre, male citizens put on a toga too. Clothes were generally made of wool or linen, but wealthy Romans could afford fine silks from China.

Wealthy women wore lots of jewellery.

Make-up

A wealthy Roman woman might spend hours getting ready in the morning. Slaves dressed their mistress's hair and applied her make-up. Pale skin was a sign of high status, so women used powered chalk or white lead on their faces to make them paler. Grey hair was sometimes dyed with a paste made from crushed earthworms!

Outfit for women

Women and girls wore a long tunic. If they were married, they also wore a floor-length dress called a stola over the top. Clothes were often brightly coloured.

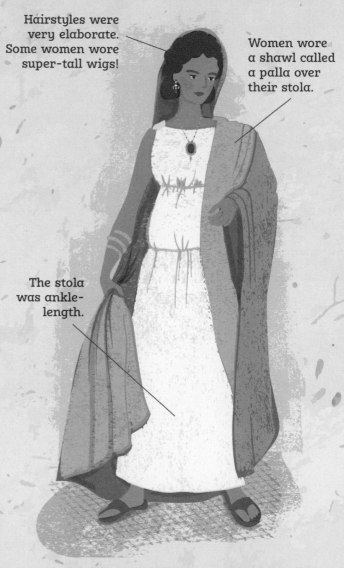

Hairstyles were very elaborate. Some women wore super-tall wigs!

Women wore a shawl called a palla over their stola.

The stola was ankle-length.

Roman underwear was a loincloth called a subligaculum. People wore this and their tunic to bed.

Everyday outfit for men

Day-to-day clothing for men was a knee-length tunic. This was worn by everyone from rich Romans to slaves.

Beards become fashionable around 130 CE. Before then, most Roman men were clean-shaven. They went to the barber every day for a shave.

In cold weather, men might wear an extra tunic and a cloak.

A short-sleeved tunic was tied with a belt.

Sandals were made of leather in different styles.

Formal outfit for men

Only male citizens were allowed to wear a toga. This was a long piece of cloth worn draped around the body. It would have been hot and sweaty to wear, and difficult to put on because it was so heavy.

A tunic was worn underneath the toga.

The toga was worn draped over the left shoulder.

Togas were white and made from wool. Important officials wore tunics and togas with a purple stripe.

The emperor's clothes

By law, only the emperor was allowed to dress entirely in purple. Purple dye was made from the crushed shells of the *Murex* sea snail and was very expensive. Instead of a crown, the emperor sometimes wore a wreath of laurel leaves.

GETTING AROUND

A huge network of roads criss-crossed the Roman Empire, linking cities, ports and remote frontier posts. All sorts of travellers used them: government officials, farmers and traders transporting cartloads of goods, legionaries marching from camp to camp, people heading to festivals or healing sanctuaries, and rich Romans visiting their countryside villas.

Raeda

Ordinary people might make journeys in a raeda, a simple carriage with wooden benches and sometimes a cloth roof. These carriages were often pulled by oxen or mules.

Essedum

Travellers in a hurry might choose to ride in a speedy essedum. This was a small chariot that could carry two passengers standing up.

Carpentum

Romans with more money travelled in a carpentum. This carriage wasn't any quicker, but it was more comfortable, with a wooden arched roof, more space and a suspension system that made the bumps in the road more bearable! It was often richly decorated inside, and sometimes on the outside too.

Litters

In cities, most people got around on foot, but wealthy Romans were sometimes carried in a litter instead. This was a sort of portable bed, carried by slaves.

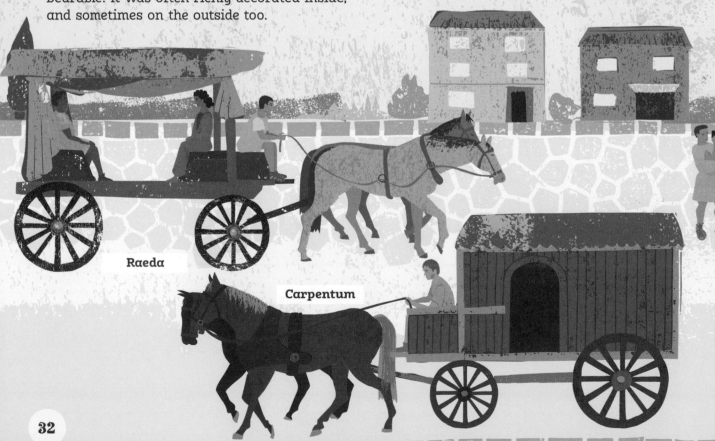

Raeda

Carpentum

Roman road building

The 50,000 miles (80,000km) of paved roads built by the Romans were one of their greatest achievements. Many of these long, straight roads are still used today! They were built by the Roman army to move troops and equipment quickly around the Empire. Here's how they were constructed:

1 Trench filled with large stones.

2 Layer of pebbles and sand.

3 Layer of cement.

4 Paving stones laid on top.

5 Ditches on either side for water drainage.

Travellers broke their journeys at simple roadside inns along the main roads. Rich Romans could stay at one of their countryside villas instead.

Litter

Essedum

On the road

Travel by road was slow and uncomfortable. A journey that takes an hour today would have taken days back then. Travellers also had to put up with the noisy clatter of the carriage's iron-rimmed wooden wheels on the paved roads.

LIFE IN THE ARMY

The Roman army was a fearsome fighting machine that was well-armed, disciplined and highly trained. A job in the army offered good perks, especially if you were poor. But it also meant hard physical work and long years spent far away from home.

Legionaries and auxiliaries

The army was made up of foot soldiers called legionaries, who were all citizens. These were helped by non-citizen soldiers called auxiliaries, who usually came from lands conquered by the Romans. Auxiliaries sometimes fought on horseback or as archers or stone-slingers.

On the move

When they were on the move, soldiers had to march up to 20 miles (30km) a day, carrying heavy packs. At the end of the day, there was no time to relax. Instead, they were set to work building a new camp for the night. This was surrounded by a ditch and a fence of sharp wooden stakes. The next day, the poor soldiers had to get up and do it all over again!

Training and tactics

Constant training meant that soldiers were always ready for battle. They practised hand-to-hand combat daily and kept fit by swimming, marching and running. The men also learnt battle tactics. In the testudo (or 'tortoise') formation, they formed a small group and raised their shields to protect them, just like a tortoise shell.

A legionary's kit

Soldiers had to buy their own equipment, which they carried in a pack on a stick. Packs could weigh more than 88lbs (40kg), about the same as an average 12-year-old!

Soldiers had to serve for at least 25 years. On retirement, legionaries were given a gift of land or money and auxiliaries were rewarded with Roman citizenship.

A soldier's life

Roman soldiers didn't spend all their time fighting in wars. For long periods, the Roman Empire was at peace. During these times, the army guarded the territories they had conquered, and built roads, bridges, forts and aqueducts. Soldiers also spent a lot of time training, so they stayed fit and ready for battle.

Throwing spear (pilum)

Helmet to protect the head and the back of the neck but still allow soldiers to hear and see

Armour made of overlapping metal strips, so soldiers could bend and move

Dagger (pugio)

Large, curved wooden shield to protect the body

Short sword (gladius) for stabbing

Sandals with iron studs on the soles

Officers called centurions wore helmets with a crest, so they could be easily seen on the battlefield.

35

ENTERTAINMENT

The Romans loved to be entertained! Chariot races, theatre performances and gory gladiator fights all drew large, excited crowds. These shows were put on during special festivals called ludi (which means 'games'), and were free to everyone, rich and poor.

Gladiator shows

Gruesome gladiator fights and wild beast shows were held at a big arena called an amphitheatre. Most gladiators were slaves or prisoners who were forced to fight, but some were volunteers hoping to win fame and glory – the best gladiators could become heroes and earn a lot of money. There were different types of gladiators, with different weapons and armour. Most gladiators were men, but there were a few women too.

Wild animal shows featured bears, panthers, lions and other exotic animals captured from all around the Empire. These poor animals were killed in their hundreds in bloodthirsty staged 'hunts', where they fought each other or armed fighters called venatores. The Romans also sometimes threw prisoners into the arena to be eaten.

If a gladiator lost a fight, the emperor had the power to spare their life, or end it, by turning his thumb down or up.

Crested helmet with grille to protect the face

Short sword (gladius)

Padded arm guard (manica)

Large oblong shield

Murmillo gladiator

Theatre

Romans enjoyed watching all kinds of plays. There were comedies and tragedies, performed by male actors wearing elaborate masks, as well as a type of theatre called mime. This was acted by women as well as men, without masks, and the stories were often pretty rude!

Theatre masks

Chariot races

For many Romans, nothing beat the excitement of a day at the races. The sport was fast, exciting and very dangerous. Drivers (called 'charioteers') raced their chariots, pulled by two or four horses, around an oblong racetrack called a circus. If they made the slightest slip-up, their chariot might crash and be smashed to pieces, and them with it!

In Rome, there were four chariot racing teams: the Greens, Reds, Blues and Whites. Every Roman had a favourite team – a bit like football fans today.

The Colosseum

The Colosseum in Rome opened in 80 CE and is still standing today. This huge amphitheatre could fit 50,000 people inside and was the most impressive arena in the whole of the Roman Empire.

Women and poor people sat in the top levels.

Gladiators' entrance to the arena

Rich, important men sat in the lower seats, with the best views.

Trapdoors led to small underground rooms, where wild animals were kept.

Canvas was stretched out on poles to provide shade.

The emperor watched from an exclusive viewing box right next to the action.

80 entrances at street level gave easy access to seats.

The floor was covered with sand to soak up blood.

MAKE A THEATRE MASK

The masks that actors wore had exaggerated expressions to make it easy for the audience to tell what sort of character they were playing, even from far away. Masks also allowed actors to switch easily between playing different characters. Have a go at designing your own Roman mask.

You will need

- **A4 (letter-sized) thick card**
- **Pencil**
- **Scissors**
- **Glue**
- **Yarn**
- **Colouring pens or pencils**
- **2 pieces of string,** 4¾in (12cm) long

1 Draw the outline of your mask onto the card and cut it out with scissors.

2 Hold the mask up to your face and use a pencil to mark where your eyes are. Draw the eye and mouth holes and cut them out. Different shaped holes can make different expressions.

3 Now decorate your mask. Make a nose from a triangle of card, folded in half. Draw features like eyebrows. Use yarn to add hair or a beard. The mask shown above has a laurel wreath made from card. Add two holes at the sides, for the string.

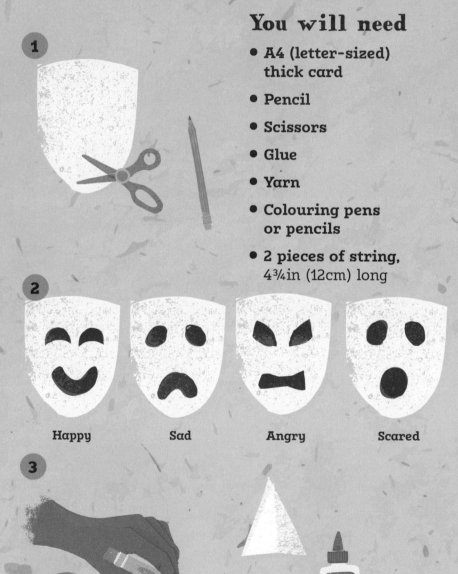

1

2

Happy   Sad   Angry   Scared

3

Roman theatres were usually semicircles, with a raised stage and elaborate stage backdrop.

MAKE PANPIPES

The Romans listened to music in lots of different places – during festivals, at dinner parties and in religious ceremonies. Some of the instruments that the Romans played, like horns, cymbals and panpipes, are still played today.

1

You will need

- **8 extra-wide (smoothie or boba) paper straws**
- **Ruler**
- **Scissors**
- **Card**
- **Craft glue**

1 Carefully cut the straws to the following lengths: 7in (17.5cm), 6in (15.5cm), 5¼in (13.5cm), 5in (12.5cm), 4¼in (11cm), 4in (10cm), 3½in (9cm) and 3¼in (8.5cm).

2 On a piece of card, draw around the end of a straw to create 8 small circles. Cut them out and glue one onto the end of each straw. Blocking off the ends of your straws like this will make your panpipes sound better when you play them!

3 Line up the straws from longest to shortest, with the open ends all in a straight line. Glue a long strip of card all the way round the straws, to hold them together.

2

3

To play your panpipes, try to blow across the tops of the pipes, not down into them.

AT THE CHARIOT RACES

Today my master has allowed me to come to the chariot races for the first time, with Felix and Gallio. I'm so excited I could burst! It seems like all of the city has turned up to watch. I can see flashes of red, blue and green in the crowd. Gallio tells me that's because some people have dressed in the colours of their favourite team. Felix says he's sure the Greens will win the first race and he disappears to make a bet. Gallio laughs and says Felix might as well throw his money away, as there's no way the Greens can win when the great charioteer Diocles is racing for the Reds.

It's almost time for the first race to start! I look over to the starting gates, where eight chariots are lined up, each one pulled by two huge horses, snorting and stamping their feet. Gallio points out Diocles, and I watch as he and the other charioteers climb into the wobbling chariots and tie the reins around their waists. Some of them look a bit nervous.

A man holds up a white cloth and the crowd grows quiet. When he drops the cloth, a horn sounds and the gates spring open – they're off! Around me, the crowd roars as the horses thunder down the track, leaving thick clouds of dust billowing behind them. The noise of shouting and galloping hooves is so loud it hurts my ears.

For the next fifteen minutes I don't take my eyes off the racetrack for a single second. Round and round the chariots hurtle, jolting and bouncing over bumps in the track. In the fourth lap, Diocles's chariot almost collides with another but he manages to veer away at the last moment. Phew! By the sixth lap, Diocles is in third place. Come on, I urge him, only one more lap to go!

Now it's the final lap, and the Blue charioteer in second place is trying to cut in front of the Green charioteer in the lead. For a moment it looks like he will make it . . . but suddenly there's a loud crack as his wheel collides with the central barrier. He whips out his knife and cuts his reins, tumbling to the ground as his chariot splinters into a thousand pieces around him! The other chariots swerve to avoid him and the rearing, panicked horses. Is he dead? No, he's rolled over and is staggering up, covered in blood.

The other chariots are thundering towards the finish line now and the crowd is roaring louder than ever. The Green charioteer is still in the lead, but Diocles is gaining on him, quickly. Now they're neck and neck! With a final crack of his whip, Diocles sweeps past and crosses the finish line, raising his fist in victory. The crowd go wild! Beside me, Gallio is shouting and dancing. Felix looks fed up. I shout Diocles's name until my voice goes hoarse. Once he was a slave boy like me, and now look – he is a hero! Maybe when I grow up I will become a charioteer and the crowds will chant my name, too.

RELIGION

The Romans believed in hundreds of different gods and goddesses. They thought these gods had power over every part of their lives, from protecting their homes and helping crops to grow, to healing them when they were sick. This meant it was very important to keep them happy!

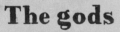

Minerva

The gods

There was a god for just about everything in ancient Rome. As well as the main gods, there were lesser gods for all sorts of things that were important to daily life, from bees to bread-making. There was even a goddess of door hinges and a god of manure! The Romans also sometimes borrowed gods from the lands they conquered, like Mithras from Persia and Isis from Egypt. Some Roman emperors were made into gods when they died, too.

The main gods

Jupiter: god of the sky and king of the gods

Juno: Jupiter's wife and the goddess of women

Neptune: god of the sea

Mars: god of war

Venus: goddess of love

Minerva: goddess of wisdom and crafts

Mercury: god of travellers and merchants

Temples and worship

To honour the gods, the Romans prayed and made offerings at temples and shrines every day. Gifts of honey, cake, oil, coins or jewellery were offered, and sometimes animals were sacrificed. Some gods also had special festival days held in their honour.

Omens and superstitions

Have you ever crossed your fingers for good luck, or avoided walking under a ladder? The Romans were even more superstitious! They believed in omens – signs from the gods that a good or bad thing was going to happen. A bad omen might make a superstitious Roman change their plans completely.

People called augurs looked for good or bad omens by studying the flight and behaviour of birds. The army even kept cages of sacred chickens and watched the way they ate before going into battle.

After an animal was sacrificed, a priest studied its organs to see what the message from the gods was.

Many Romans wore lucky charms called amulets to protect them from bad fortune. Children were given amulets at birth.

Some Romans believed their dreams could tell the future.

Some Romans believed in werewolves, witches, vampires and other evil spirits.

Christianity

From the 1st century CE, a new religion, Christianity, began to spread around the Empire. Christians refused to worship the Roman gods, and were sometimes punished for their beliefs. Things changed in the 4th century, when Constantine became Rome's first Christian emperor. In 380 CE, Christianity became the official religion of the Roman Empire.

Thunderstorms were thought to be a bad omen.

Several months are named after Roman gods, including March (Mars), June (Juno) and January (Janus – the two-faced god of beginnings).

MEDICINE

Treatments for the sick in ancient Rome were a mix of medicine and magic! Many people believed disease was caused by the gods or curses. Sick people took herbal medicines prescribed by doctors, but would also pray to the gods to help them get well.

Roman doctors

Most of the doctors in ancient Rome were Greek, and some became very rich and famous. Medicines were made from herbs and plants, which were ground up by pharmacists into pills or ointments. Doctors could perform simple operations, but surgery was always a last resort because it was so risky. It would have been agonizingly painful too – there was no anaesthetic in Roman times.

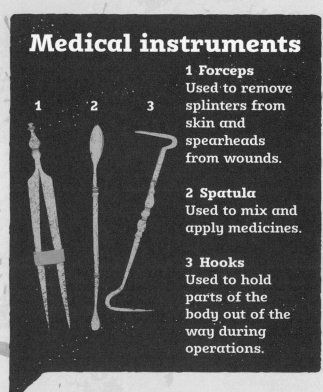

Medical instruments

1 2 3

1 Forceps
Used to remove splinters from skin and spearheads from wounds.

2 Spatula
Used to mix and apply medicines.

3 Hooks
Used to hold parts of the body out of the way during operations.

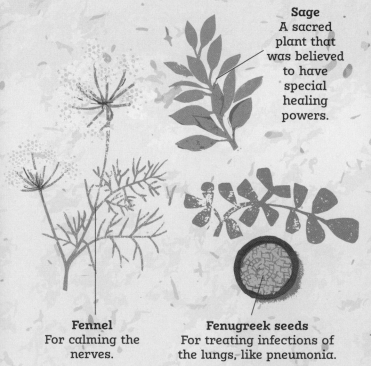

Sage
A sacred plant that was believed to have special healing powers.

Fennel
For calming the nerves.

Fenugreek seeds
For treating infections of the lungs, like pneumonia.

Shrines and superstition

Sick Romans might travel to a healing shrine to pray to the gods. Some Romans spent the night at the sanctuary of the healing god Asclepius, where they hoped a cure would be revealed to them in a dream. Others turned to magic spells or tried bizarre remedies, such as kissing a donkey's nose to cure a cold!

Romans probably had very healthy teeth, because they didn't eat much sugar.

Remembering the dead

Romans buried their dead in cemeteries outside the city or town walls. Many tombstones had inscriptions called epitaphs that described the person and what they did for a living. The sandals carved into this tombstone show that the man used to be a shoemaker. People sometimes kept wax masks of their dead relatives and ancestors on display in their house.

Early childhood was a risky time in ancient Rome — only half of all children made it to their tenth birthday.

Keeping clean

The Romans realised how important hygiene was in preventing the spread of disease. They built huge aqueducts to carry fresh water into cities, and state-of-the-art sewers to take away the waste. There were public baths where people could clean themselves, and plenty of public toilets flushed by running water. Impressive stuff!

Just how hygienic were these places? Perhaps not very. The warm, moist baths would have been a breeding ground for infection, and some historians think the public toilets would have been pretty filthy.

FOOD AND DRINK

Food in Roman times wasn't all stuffed nightingales, flamingo tongues and honey-drizzled dormice. Some very wealthy Romans did eat like this, at least some of the time, but the food that most people ate was very simple and didn't vary much from one day to the next.

Where Romans ate

The simple apartments that many ordinary Romans lived in had no kitchen, so people mostly ate out. Snack bars called thermopolia had a counter facing the street for takeaway hot food, and sometimes a room inside where customers could sit at tables to eat.

Only rich Roman households had kitchens. Here, slaves cooked food in clay ovens and in pots hung over an open fire. Meals were served in a lavish room called the triclinium, which had three couches arranged around low tables (see pages 48–49).

When Romans ate

Lentaculum: A simple breakfast eaten at sunrise – a piece of bread, which might be dipped in honey or wine.

Prandium: A small lunch of bread and cheese, eaten around midday.

Cena: Dinner was the main meal and was eaten mid-afternoon. In a wealthy Roman's house, this sociable meal would last until evening.

Jars of food and wine were set into holes in the counter of the thermopolium.

What Romans ate

Ordinary Romans ate quite simple food: a lot of vegetables, olive oil, bread, beans and cheese, washed down with watered-down wine. Fish and meat were more expensive, so were mainly eaten by the wealthy. The very poorest Romans mostly survived on a simple porridge called 'puls', which was made from barley or other grains mixed with water.

Lots of recipes used a stinky, salty sauce called garum, made from rotting fish guts.

Olives were eaten but also pressed to make oil used for cooking, cleaning the skin and in oil lamps.

Herbs were used to flavour dishes.

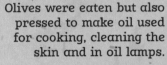

Garum

Olives

Figs

Fish

Pears

Bread

Walnuts

Oysters

Mint and thyme

Cheese

Dessert was fresh fruit, sometimes drenched with honey.

Carrots

Asparagus

Eggs

Honeycomb

Beans

Romans ate the eggs of many different birds, not just chickens.

Roman banquets

Wealthy Romans threw dinner parties that could last for hours and include six or more courses, each with several dishes. Guests would be treated to seafood and meat, such as oysters, wild boar, songbirds and suckling pig. To show off, hosts might serve exotic delicacies such as giraffe legs or ostrich brains. Guests would be entertained with music, dancing or poetry.

AT A BANQUET

Tonight, the master is hosting a dinner party. The kitchen has been bustling with activity since dawn, and Anthus, the cook, has been in a very bad mood. He's been barking out orders all day and grumbling about how much there is to do – vegetables to chop, songbirds to pluck and stuff, wild boar to roast, lobsters to boil, fish to fetch from the market . . .

At least I managed to stay out of his way. I was set to work polishing the silver cups and plates until they shone. My mother told me that one of the guests is an important man, so the master has hired the best musicians and asked Anthus to prepare peacock tongues – he must really want to impress him!

My job tonight is to wash the guests' hands in between courses. When the guests start to arrive I make my way to the triclinium, holding a bowl of perfumed water and a towel. There's a soft glow from the oil lamps and the air smells faintly of rose petals, which my mother scattered on the floor earlier. Over on one side of the room, musicians are standing ready with their flutes and lyres. The important guest is shown to his couch – the best one in the room, in the middle. Everyone looks very grand, with their gleaming white togas, brightly coloured dresses and sparkling jewellery. Soon, Felix begins to serve the wine – hot and spiced for some, sweetened with honey or cooled with snow for others.

When the dishes for the first course are brought in, my mouth waters! There are plump oysters and spiky sea urchins, sliced eggs smothered with sauce, and juicy snails that have been soaking in milk in the kitchen for days. As the guests eat, I listen to their conversations. Most of it is boring talk about the law courts and gossip about neighbours but I prick up my ears when talk turns to a new batch of gladiators that will be fighting next week – I wish I could see them!

The second course is even more splendid than the first. The face of the important guest lights up when he sees the peacock tongues. He picks one up with his fingers and gulps it down, murmuring his appreciation and smacking his greasy lips. The master looks very pleased. Next comes a plate of figs smothered in honey, pears, custards and candied dates. One of the guests looks a bit pale. I hope they're not going to be sick, or I'll be the one clearing it up.

It's getting late now. The sun has gone down long ago, my feet are hurting and I'm trying hard not to yawn. Finally, the guests begin to leave, unsteady on their feet after so much wine. Soon I am unrolling my sleeping mat and slipping gratefully into bed.

ROMAN RECIPES

We know quite a lot about what the Romans ate and drank — they even left behind a cookbook, full of recipes! Do you think you would have enjoyed eating like an ancient Roman? Try out these Roman-inspired recipes and see.

Honey cake

Honey cakes were a popular sweet treat in ancient Rome. Back then, there was no baking powder, which we use today to make cakes rise, and no sugar either. Instead, the Romans used honey for sweetness, and introduced lots of air into the cake batter by beating the eggs very hard. That's what you're going to do in this recipe too.

Ingredients

- 3 eggs
- 5oz (150g) runny honey
- 5oz (150g) plain flour

1 Preheat the oven to 340°F (170°C). Grease a cake tin and line it with baking paper.

2 Crack the eggs into a bowl and whisk them until they are very frothy, with lots of air bubbles.

3 Continue whisking while you add the honey, a little at a time.

4 Sieve the flour into the mixture and fold it in very gently. You want to try to keep all the air you have whisked in.

5 Bake in the oven for around 45 minutes, until a toothpick or skewer comes out clean. Serve warm, drizzled with more honey.

Bee keeping

Bees were very important to the Romans. Honey was used in lots of recipes, and beeswax was used to make writing tablets (see page 24).

Roman salad

This dish is based on a recipe written by a Roman soldier and farmer called Columella.

Ingredients

- 1oz (25g) each of fresh mint, coriander and parsley
- Half a small leek, finely sliced
- A big handful of rocket leaves
- Handful of chopped walnuts
- 3½oz (100g) firm goat's cheese or feta, crumbled
- 3 tbsp olive oil
- 1 tbsp red wine vinegar
- Black pepper

1 First pick the leaves off the herbs, then use a pestle and mortar to crush up the herbs, leek and rocket. If you don't have one, you can bash them in a plastic bowl using the end of rolling pin instead.

2 Sprinkle the walnuts and crumbled goat's cheese over the salad.

3 Mix together the oil, vinegar and pepper to make the dressing, and pour it over.

The ancient Roman cookbook Apicius contains hundreds of recipes for everything from salads to boiled parrot.

Posca

While rich Romans got to enjoy the finest wines, the common people and the army had to make do with a drink called posca. This was made from poor-quality wine that tasted a bit like vinegar.

1 In a glass, dissolve the honey in a small amount of hot water.

2 Add the vinegar and cold water. Your posca is ready to drink!

Ingredients

- 2 tbsp honey
- 9 fl oz (250ml) cold water
- 2 tbsp red wine vinegar

COULD YOU HAVE LIVED LIKE A ROMAN?

In some ways, the Roman way of life wasn't so different to ours. In cities, people could eat out, go to the theatre, cheer on their favourite team at a huge stadium, and hang out with their friends at bathhouses that were a bit like our leisure centres. But in other ways, Romans lived quite differently to us. Think about the questions here and talk about your answers with a friend, parent, carer or teacher.

1 At school, young children studied reading, writing and arithmetic. There were no opportunities for being creative, and lessons were generally learnt 'by rote', which means by repeating them over and over again. Teachers were very strict too, so there was no chatting in class! How do Roman lessons compare to lessons in your school?

2 If you time-travelled back to Roman times, what three things would you miss the most from your modern-day life? It might be certain gadgets, toys or foods, or even something simple like toilet paper. Is there anything you'd like to take from the time of the Romans and bring back to the modern world?

3 One of the most prized skills in ancient Rome was the art of speaking well, called rhetoric. It was so important it was taught to older boys at school. How good do you think you would have been at giving speeches and persuading your Roman listeners? Test yourself in front of your family or friends by arguing the case for one of the following:

- Giving Roman women the vote
- Getting rid of slavery
- Banning wild beast shows.

4 Guests at Roman dinner parties expected to be entertained. A host might arrange musicians or dancers, storytellers, poetry readers, actors, magicians, acrobats or sometimes even trained wild animals like leopards! If you were hosting a Roman dinner party, what entertainment would you choose?

5 The Romans had lots of different gods for all the things that were important in their lives, from fruit trees to sewers. Make up three new Roman gods or goddesses for things that are important to you – for example, you might have a god of books or a goddess of football or friendship. Give your new gods names.

6 Wealthy Romans relied on slaves to do almost everything for them, from cooking their food and dressing them to walking their children to school. Make a list of all the little jobs in your house that, in Roman times, would have been done by slaves. How many jobs can you think of? Which people or machines do these jobs now?

7 There wasn't much privacy in ancient Rome. Many families lived and slept in poky apartments (or even a single room), while rich Romans spent their lives surrounded by ever-present slaves. People ate together, washed together, and sometimes even went to the toilet together! How would you feel about living in this way?

8 Just like today, people living in ancient Rome lived very different lives depending on their circumstances. Which of the following would you rather be?

- A soldier living in a fort on the frontier, in Europe or Africa.
- A craftsperson living above their shop in Rome.
- A chariot driver – a risky job, but with the chance to become rich and famous.
- A trusted slave who is treated well, almost like one of the family.
- A wealthy woman – life is easy, but you're not allowed to vote or hold any position of power, and you didn't get to choose who you married.

GLOSSARY

aqueduct
A channel used for bringing water into towns and cities. The channel could be underground or raised up on arches.

amphitheatre
Oval open-air arena used for staging gladiator fights and other public shows.

archaeologist
A person who studies how humans lived in the past by looking at the things they left behind, such as pottery, tools and buildings.

barbarian
The name the Romans gave to groups of people living outside the Empire. Sometimes, the Romans fought wars against barbarian tribes. Other times, they made alliances with them or recruited them as soldiers.

brazier
A container for burning charcoal, used for cooking and heating.

centurion
Army officer who commanded a unit of 80 men called a century.

chamber pot
A bowl kept in the bedroom and used as a toilet at night.

chariot
Two-wheeled vehicle pulled by horses.

circus
Long stadium where chariot races were held.

citizen
A person who belongs to a state, and has certain rights and privileges. In Ancient Rome, the rules about who could be a citizen changed over time.

consul
One of the most important senators in the Senate. At any one time, there were two consuls, who were elected to serve for a year.

dictator
A ruler who has total power. In the Republic, a dictator could be appointed by the Senate to rule in emergencies. In 49 BCE, the Roman general Julius Caesar made himself a dictator.

emperor
The ruler of an empire.

empire
A large area of different lands and peoples, all ruled by one person or government.

estate
A large farm, mostly worked by slaves. Roman farming estates grew crops such as wheat, olives and grapes, and kept cows and goats for milk and cheese, and bees for honey.

fort
A well-protected building or group of buildings where soldiers live. Many Roman soldiers lived in forts on the frontiers (edges) of the Empire, keeping watch for invaders. Over time, some of these forts turned into small towns.

furnace
A structure where fuel such as wood is burned, to make heat.

gladiator
Trained fighter who fought in shows held at an amphitheatre. There were different types of gladiator, such as the retiarius (armed with a trident and net) and the heavily armoured murmillo.

Gaul
The name given by the Romans to the region of Europe that is roughly the same area of modern-day France, Belgium, northern Italy and western Germany.

hygiene
The practice of keeping clean to stay healthy and free of disease.

insulae
Blocks of flats, several stories high, where most people in Roman cities lived. The bottom floor, at street level, often housed shops.

legionary
A Roman foot soldier. The Roman army was arranged into units: 80 legionaries made up a century; six centuries grouped together (480 men) made up a cohort; and ten cohorts grouped together (4,800 men) made up a legion.

mosaic
A pattern or picture made by arranging small tiles of stone, glass or other material. Many Roman houses and public buildings were decorated with mosaics.

Persia
The region of southwestern Asia that is roughly the area of modern-day Iran.

Roman Republic
The period of ancient Rome from 509 BCE to 27 BCE, when Rome was governed by elected officials, including consuls and senators in the Senate.

Roman Empire
The period of ancient Rome from 27 BCE to 476 CE, when Rome was governed by emperors. The Senate still existed during this time, but it lost its power and did what it was told by the emperor.

Senate
The governing assembly of Rome, made up of important and wealthy men called senators.

slave
A woman, man or child who is owned as property by someone else, and made to work.

sundial
An instrument that tells the time of day by the position of a shadow cast on the surface of the sundial, which has markings for each hour of daylight.

temple
A building where a god or gods are worshipped. In ancient Rome, sacrifices to the gods were performed outside the temple. Generally, only priests were allowed inside.

thermopolium
Snack bar selling drinks and hot food, used by Romans who weren't able to cook in their own homes.

toga
Piece of clothing worn by male Roman citizens. The toga was a status symbol, worn at public events.

villa
The countryside house of rich Romans. Some were very luxurious, containing many rooms, courtyards, landscaped gardens, pools and baths.

ABOUT THE AUTHOR

Claire Saunders has been writing and editing books for more than 20 years. Specialising in children's non-fiction, she has authored or co-authored many titles including *The Power Book*, *The Birthday Almanac*, *A World of Gratitude* and various activity books, including *The Great British Staycation Activity Book*, the *Football Fantastic Activity Book* and the *Only in America Activity Book*. A graduate of Cambridge University, she has previously worked for Ivy Press and Rough Guides and still loves travelling the world, learning about the history of other cultures. She lives with her family in Lewes, southern England.

Acknowledgements
Thanks to Professor Matthew Nicholls for his expert knowledge and help.

First published 2023 by Button Books, an imprint of Guild of Master Craftsman Publications Ltd, Castle Place, 166 High Street, Lewes, East Sussex, BN7 1XU, UK. Text © Claire Saunders, 2023. Copyright in the Work © GMC Publications Ltd, 2023. ISBN 978 1 78708 126 0. Distributed by Publishers Group West in the United States. All rights reserved. The right of Claire Saunders to be identified as the author of this work has been asserted in accordance with the Copyright, Designs and Patents Act 1988, sections 77 and 78. No part of this publication may be reproduced, stored in a retrieval system, or transmitted in any form or by any means without the prior permission of the publisher and copyright owner. The publishers and author can accept no legal responsibility for any consequences arising from the application of information, advice, or instructions given in this publication. A catalogue record for this book is available from the British Library. Publisher: Jonathan Bailey, Production: Jim Bulley, Senior Project Editor: Virginia Brehaut, Designer: Robin Shields, Illustrator: Ruth Hickson. Colour origination by GMC Reprographics. Printed and bound in China.

FSC
www.fsc.org
MIX
Paper | Supporting responsible forestry
FSC® C020056

For more on Button Books, contact:
GMC Publications Ltd, Castle Place,
166 High Street, Lewes, East Sussex,
BN7 1XU, United Kingdom
Tel: +44 (0)1273 488005
buttonbooks.co.uk/buttonbooks.us

Button Books